T0365868

Creative Recycling

HANDMADE IN AFRICA

Jude Andreasen & Cleve Overton

To order additional copies of this book, contact:
Xlibris
844-714-8691
www.Xlibris.com
Orders@Xlibris.com

ISBN: 978-1-4134-6188-6 (sc)
ISBN: 978-1-4134-6191-6 (hc)
ISBN: 978-1-4771-7827-0 (e)

Library of Congress Control Number: 2004095159

Print information available on the last page

Rev. date: 02/21/2022

This photographic book documents a delightfull collection of handmade miniature vehicles, boats and planes made from discarded and recycled material in Africa and purchased in at least 20 different countries between 1985 and 2003. They range from rudimentary to amazingly sophisticated. The collection has educational, cultural and environmental aspects, and the pieces showcase the imagination and ingenuity of African children and craftsmen. Author and collector Jude Andreasen spent eight years working and living in African countries. Cleve Overton has traveled the continent with Ms. Andreasen from the Cape to Cairo.

Preface

We bought our first handmade miniature African vehicle in 1985 on the streets of Kinshasa, Zaire (now the Democratic Republic ofthe Congo). In later years and other countries, we could never resist buying more. Friends working in different African countries contributed to an ever-growing collection, which now includes about 300 pieces. The majority of the pieces are from West African countries, where we spent the longest time. The pieces in this collection were purchased in Benin, Burkina Faso, Cameroon, Cap Verde, Congo, Cote d'Ivoire, Democratic Republic of the Congo, Gambia, Ghana, Kenya, Madagascar, Malawi, Mali, Mauritania, Nigeria, Senegal, South Africa, Sao Tome, Togo, Uganda, Zambia and Zimbabwe. While most are by unknown craftsmen, a few are signed, such as the bicycles and vehicles by Iba Diop of Senegal. A large tanker truck from concentrated milk cans was made by Malian Ladji Badiaga. In a few cases, the artist/craftsman himself was the seller, as in the case of Andrew Maphanga, who made the intricate gold wire motorcycle sculpture we purchased in Capetown, South Africa.

Introduction

We got the idea for sharing the collection by publishing it when we first saw the book, **Recycled/Re-Seen: Folk Art from the Global Scrap Heap**, a collection of essays on folk art made from trash. **Recycled/Re-Seen** documents a traveling exhibit mounted in 1996 by the Museum of International Folk Art in Sante Fe, New Mexico, and uses the word "recyclia" to characterize art made from discarded materials. A particular quote from the book made us see a theme for our collection, "From ancient times, children have been fascinated by vehicles. Greek and Roman boys played with miniature carts they made by hand. And not surprisingly, mechanized transport still fascinates and stirs the creativity of children throughout the world who manipulate their found trash and treasures to create planes, buses, bikes, trucks, tractors, cars and canoes." **Recycled/Re-Seen** features folk art from many countries, but the authors chose a miniature car made in Mali for the cover. Our collection has been almost exclusively such African recyclia.

An African child's car may be a tin can and a string, or a cardboard box with tin cans for wheels

While each piece can be categorized by the country in which it was purchased, the skills and inspiration that went into their creation knows no borders. Craftsmen who perfect their skills in one country travel to neighboring countries and learn from each other, so it can be difficult to determine the origin of a piece by its looks. Most of the wire toys in the collection are from the central and southern African countries. The pieces we bought in Zaire in the Eighties were gray wire held together with thinner copper wire, and many of the wire sculptures found on South Africa's sidewalks are from Zimbabwe. In the semi-arid and desert countries of Senegal and Mali, trees are scarce and most miniature vehicles are made from tin cans. Wooden pieces are from countries which still have forests, like Cote d'Ivoire and Cameroon, but they are sometimes brought to Senegal to be sold. In the absence of other material, some youngsters use clay to model vehicles.

There is no word for "toy" in most African languages. African children have to squeeze play time in between family chores. It is common to see a young girl carrying her toddler sibling on her back or a bucket of water on her head, or a young boy carrying a load of firewood or hay bigger than he is. In her few spare moments, a girl may make a doll out of rags, but some girls and most boys will eventually make something with wheels. All children love things that roll, even an old tire they can push with a stick. The children are creative and imaginative despite the scarcity of materials and tools. In Niamey, Accra, Lomé, Cotonou, Kinshasa, Kikwit, Dakar, Abidjan, Nouakchott, Ouagadougou, Nairobi and any place in between, you will see children with vehicles made of discarded material. Asked what it is, the child will reply that it is a "car" or "truck," never a toy.

An adolescent may fashion one for a younger sibling while dreaming of owning a car or becoming a pilot. For tires, they use cut up rubber sandals, caps from brake fluid or aerosol cans, or strips of inner tubes wrapped around wire. Insecticide cans are especially popular, showing insects and words like Doom, Yotox, Rambo, Danger and Poison. Teenagers and young men recognize that such handmade vehicles appeal to foreign aid workers, Peace Corps volunteers and tourists who will buy them. In countries where unemployment is high, they can earn an income by perfecting their craft. They use care and precision to add doors that open, wheels that turn and other moving parts that so resemble a full-size vehicle that the buyer cannot resist. They use glue and metal solder to make sturdier, ever more intricate pieces. In a few countries, like Ghana and Malawi, straw or *raffia* is used by clever weavers to make elaborate jeeps, sometimes with a straw engine.

Cars Rapides from Senegal

The universal appeal of vehicles is understandable. Just as teenagers in industrialized countries long for their first car, children in developing countries recognize early on the lure of an object that offers speed, power and independence. In developing countries where most adults can never hope to own one, vehicles are status symbols, and drivers are proud of their profession even if someone else owns the vehicle.

Most people in African countries use public transportation, and such vehicles are colorfully painted and adorned with mottos or prayers. In Dakar, Senegal, public transport is by ubiquitous blue and orange vans called "cars rapides." The vans are notorious for causing accidents due to the poor maintenance by some owners. Bad brakes, missing lug nuts and broken lights are common problems that jeopardize the lives of those who ride as well as those who share the road with them. No matter how dangerous they are, they are a feature of daily life in Dakar, so young inventors continue to reproduce them in charming miniatures with metal and wood.

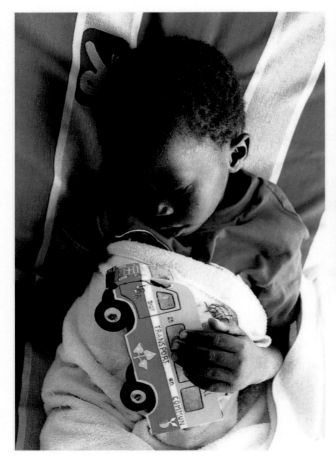

The Paris - Dakar Rally

One of the events that surely influences and inspires many African children in both the desert and the cities is the annual Paris - Dakar Rally. It began in 1978 as the Oasis Rally, launched by French racer Thierry Sabine, and continues to be a punishing marathon to this day. Daredevil drivers from many countries still compete in the annual high-risk race from Paris to Dakar through the Sahara Desert. They are followed by support trucks, jets and helicopters carrying food, water and spare parts.

When the Rally passes, village children watch in amazement as the cars, trucks and motorcycles fly over the dunes, colorfully plastered with the logos and banners of their sponsors. Children sketch cars and look for scraps of rubbish they can use to make their own miniature vehicles and stage their own mini-races. Their imaginations are stimulated by the rush and the excitement generated by the crowds of foreigners with their noisy- wheeled monsters. They compete to find colorful trash in a village where nothing is wasted.

When the racers arrive in Dakar, covered in dust, they are welcomed by cheering crowds. Rally sponsors stage an award ceremony in the center of town and the winners are acclaimed by the public and the media as triumphant road warriors.

There are dangers too. Some drivers are careless, but even careful drivers cause accidents in a wilderness where vehicles are rare and there are unseen camels in sand storms. The originator, Sabine, died when his helicopter crashed during the 1986 race. In 2003, the 25th anniversary of the rally, they skipped West Africa for the first time, citing concerns about security and terrorism. In January 2004, over 600 entrants from 40 countries participated in the 7,000 mile race, and West Africa was put back into the route at the request of competitors. West African entrepreneurs who depend upon sales to rally participants welcomed their return. Mauritania and Mali offered military guards to mitigate concerns about security. Nearly 20 jets and 30 helicopters carry the vast movable rally from staging area to staging area.

There is undoubtedly an environmental impact on the fragile desert ecosystem from the hundreds of vehicles barreling across it each year, as well as from the trash they leave behind. In 2004, organizers restricted racers to speeds of 20 miles per hour through villages to try to prevent deaths among local residents.

Tanker from Mali by Ladji Badiaga.

One prolific young entrepreneur spread hundreds of miniatures on a sidewalk outside a hotel in Antananarivo, Madagascar.

Land Rover made from reeds from Lake Malawi, lent by Agi Kiss.

Black bicycle and tricycle from the Gambia.

Cameroon's trees are so large that such trucks can typically carry only one or two logs from the forest to the port.

Logging truck by Cameroonian Mathias Tongue.

Backhoe by Mathias Tongue.

In Yaounde, Cameroon, skilled carpenter and furniture maker, Mathias Tongue, finds a lucrative side line in making miniature logging trucks.

We visited an outdoor factory in a neighborhood of Dakar called Rebeuss, where men of varying ages make lunch boxes, briefcases and trunks from used tin cans.

They also use remnants of tin rolls from local factories where tomatoes, milk and tuna fish are processed and canned. Such items are popular with tourists and sold in abundance at the Dakar airport.

Vehicles made from pesticide cans in Antananarivo, Madagascar, show the craftsman's deliberate care in centering the insect design in the middle of the car.

At a 1998 annual art festival in South Africa, we bought this anatomically-correct Harley from an Australian who said he had apprenticed to a Zimbabwean toy maker for a year.

In Togo, Peace Corps staffer Mike Fitzgerald was helping a local man support himself by buying many of the his miniatures. We bought some motorcycles from Hounkpati Komi, another craftsman in the Lomé market.

Wire beetle from South Africa.

Bicycle from Senegal by Iba Diop.

Wire motorcycle and car from Democratic Republic of the Congo.

These buses in wood and tin were made in South Africa. During the apartheid era, South Africa's black population was segregated from whites and forcefully moved from their neighborhoods to "homelands" such as Transkei. The homelands were in fragile environments with poor soil more suited to rangeland, but the black population had no choice but to farm it, resulting in severe erosion and environmental degradation. Government buses transported those who had jobs in the white factories and farms on 100-mile or more daily or weekly commutes. Workers spent much of their time away from their families on crammed buses, on which they had to pay fares from their meager salaries.

Wooden cars from Nigeria and Ghana.

A boat made from a tuna (thon in French) fish can and a replica of the ferry to Gorée Island off the coast of Dakar, Senegal, which was a holding prison for slaves before their journey to the Americas to be sold.

Replicas of the gaily-painted canoes (pirogues) used for fishing and transporting tourists in Senegal.

Concorde from Mauritania.

Wooden car from Ivory Coast (Cote d'Ivoire) with chauffeur and passenger.

Wire motorcycle from South Africa by Andrew Maphanga.

Trains from insecticide cans made in Senegal.

Bicycle from Senegal.

Push toy from Kenya.

Wooden cars from South Africa.

Postscript: Environmental Thoughts Inspired by the Collection

We initially saw the collection as educational because it was a way to teach the viewer about different African countries, as well as to show how cleverly children can improvise when they have no toys to amuse themselves. We also saw the collection as an entertaining way to promote recycling. More recently, we began to see it as a way to remind ourselves of the need to preserve clean air. Our African counterparts in the countries where we worked would say they wished they could afford a car for the status and independence it would provide.

When we began collecting these toys in the early Eighties, memories of waiting in line at gasoline stations in the Seventies were still fresh. At that time, bicycles were the primary mode of transportation in China and African capitals had few traffic jams. Twenty years later, large cities in China are banning bicycles in order to make more room for cars, and we have been appalled to see African cities increasingly clogged with cars and trucks. Gasoline internal combustion engines are still the primary mechanism of power. In most developing countries where regulatory control of emissions is lax or non-existent, gasoline still contains lead.

We believe industrialized and affluent nations have a responsibility to develop and promote alternative fuel sources and technology to reduce atmospheric pollution. The current trend in the U.S. is toward bigger and better sports utility vehicles and gas burning recreational vehicles for use on land, snow and water. Hybrid cars exist but their appeal is limited. Research on alternative fuels has not kept pace with the rising demand for vehicles, and concerns about global warming and dependence on foreign oil do not seem to be sufficiently compelling to make such research a priority.

Long before the day comes that everyone on the planet who wants a car actually has one, the availability of alternative fuels and combustion technology will be essential to ensuring clean air globally. Although global warming and what to do about it continues to be debated on an international scale, there is no disagreement that vehicle emissions contribute to the "greenhouse gas" effect.

One last thought is that recycling may be a mixed blessing. In developing countries, reusable containers are highly valued. We saw discarded liquor bottles washed and used to package shelled peanuts for sale, and tomato cans of all sizes used to measure flour and rice. We bought coffee-to-go near the train station in Mali and the container was a cleaned concentrated milk can. Unfortunately, pesticide containers, particularly steel drums and plastic jugs, are sometimes washed and reused to store food and water, resulting in terrible poisonings. One solution is education of farmers and pesticide users, but we believe pesticide manufacturers have some obligation to ensure that the containers are returned or cannot be reused. If farmers could afford (or were provided) plastic containers for food and water, they would not be tempted to reuse pesticide containers.

Acknowledgments

Most of the pieces in this exhibition were purchased in Africa by the authors. Individual pieces were contributed by Rob Bongard, Peter Reckhaus, Moctar Toumbou, Joost Lahr, Harold and Ira van der Valk, Brian Hirsch, Mimi Wolford, Gary Steele, Joanne Winman, Walter Proper, Marybeth Souza, TJ Wyatt, Ousmane Ba, Sylva Etian, Glenn Lesak, Ned Seligman, Heidi Buss and Dave Thomas. Many thanks to Agi Kiss for the loan of the marvelous Land Rover woven from reeds from the shores of Lake Malawi. Many thanks to Kathy Lane and Barbara Andreasen for the technical and photographic assistance and to Harriet Lesser and Mimi Wolford for the editing suggestions. Particular thanks to Tchapa Tchouawou, who went out of his way to introduce me to Cameroonian craftsman Mathias Tongue. Apologies to any other person who contributed pieces whom we have forgotten to mention. Six photographs of children were borrowed from the book by Franco Merici.

This collection was exhibited at the Frostburg University Performing Arts Center in October 1995 and in the Museum of York County in Rock Hill, South Carolina from August 2001 through May 2002. York County Museum staff Nancy Crane (Director of Education/Culture and Heritage Museums) and Teresa Armour (Director of Exhibitions/Culture and Heritage Museums) created a wonderful exhibit titled "Re-Cover, Re- Imagine, Re-Adapt: Creative Recycling in Africa" and organized related activities on recycling and African culture that drew rave reviews. Photographs from the York County exhibit can be seen at http://www.yorkcounty.org/museum/re3/map.html

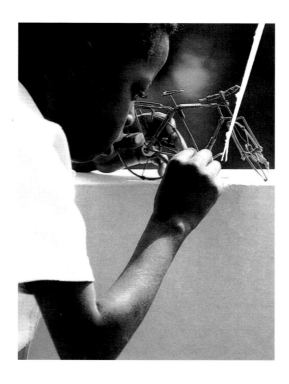

Other Resources and References on Art from Recycled Materials

Jouets d'Afrique: L'Enfance de l'Art, photographs by Franco Merici, text by Giovanna Soldini. Published by AIR AFRIQUE 1992.

Recycled/Re-Seen: Folk Art from the Global Scrap Heap
edited by C. Cerny & S. Seriff. Published by Harry N. Abrams 1996.

The Cast-Off Recast, Recycling and the Creative Transformation of Mass-Produced Objects
by Timothy C. Correll and Patrick A. Polk, editors. Published by UCLA Fowler Museum of Cultural History, Los Angeles, CA, 1999.

The Fine Art of the Tin Can by Bobby Hansson (pp 83-93) Sterling Publishing, 1996.

Galimoto by Karen Lynn Williams, Illustrated by Catherine Stock, published by Lothrup, Lee & Shephard Books of NY, a division of William Morrow & Company, 1990.

Printed in the United States
by Baker & Taylor Publisher Services